# CHRIST'S PRISON HAS NO BARS

APOSTLE ANTWAN AMEY

Scripture quotations were taken from the New International, King James Version.

For information contact; address www.ameyantwan@yahoo.com

Book and Cover design by Antwan Amey

ISBN: 13: 978-0692525340

ISBN: 10: 0692525343

# DEDICATION

I dedicate this book to my Lord and Savior Jesus Christ for being such a great God and for being so patient with me, while I am on this Christian Journey. I thank him for allowing me the opportunity to be one of his very own sons by faith through the cross at Calvary. I also thank him for allowing me to become a prisoner of his word and the agape love that he never cease to show me. Nevertheless I am grateful for the favor that he has bestowed upon my life and trusting me to be a minister of his Holy Word. I will forever proclaim the gospel of the Lord Jesus Christ whenever he tells me too or wherever I go! FOR I AM SURELY NOT ASHAMMED OF THE GOSPEL OF THE LORD JESUS CHRIST!

# #TRYCHRIST!

# CONTENTS

# CONTENTS

# PROLOGUE

To be a prisoner of Christ is to be locked down to his ways his rules and his way of life. To carry out the things of God no matter what the circumstances may be. You must continue to walk the Christian journey at any cost and any decisions that you may make must be based on Christ Jesus. When I think about a person that is locked up in any prison on earth and how no matter how bad they want a hamburger that is only ninety nine cents or even if it is free they still cannot get it. That's how I feel when it comes to the way that I live my life. Being that Christianity is not just a Sunday thing but an everyday lifestyle that we choose to live. Which brings me to understand that life is truly about choices. In the Holy Bible the Apostle Paul reminds us that we are all prisoners of Christ. With that being said this is the mindset that I believe the Lord has given me that it takes to remain on this Christian journey.

# A PRISONER OF CHRIST

Most people who are born again believers often wonder why the Christians in the Holy Bible could live out the perfect Christian race with just very little sin nature. I myself found that this was a question that I would ask myself frequently once I had gotten past the "Babe" stages in Christ or when I first found myself filled with the Holy Spirit. After all, I had received the Holy Spirit, baptized in the blood of the lamb and praying while I'm at church. But immediately following that level and the "Meat" stages begun, I found myself drifting right back to where God had delivered me from. Or a consistence fall on a week to week basis, knowing that I was not supposed to do what I knew was wrong. But Why? Was my biggest question and how is this possible? I have already been to the water, I've already been baptized and I've already been converted. How is this sin nature risen back up in my life at such a busy state? Then I begin to think well maybe I'm not really converted. Or maybe I'm just not fit for the kingdom of God or just maybe God called me but I was not one of his chosen. Then out of nowhere I remembered that the Apostle Paul had quoted that when he said that he was going to stop doing something he would always end up doing that very thing and the things that he said he was going to do, he would end up not doing those things (Romans 7:19). Yet the Holy Bible would still repeat that God is not pleased with our sins. Most chapters in the Holy Bible would all speak against the things that we were not supposed to do, but how? I then recognized that when I am fasting and praying I do not get an opportunity to really get into a lot of the sins of my choice. In fact when sin comes to my mind I cast it out and pray, or bring it down under Christ subjection, meaning I would think about what it is that Christ has to say about this very thing that I am thinking about doing. That's when I realized that God is very near and close. Maybe that's why the Bible states that man should always fast and pray! My ears are always inclined to the voice of God during this time of fasting and praying and I always hear the Lord tell me what I should not do when I'm about to make the wrong move at this time. Which would lead me to this next point which is to recognize that we have to remember that God is around us at all times and watching our every move. Also, he is trying to direct our footsteps but what we have to keep in mind is that we are prisoners of Christ! (Ephesians 3:1-4:1, Philemon 1:1) Which means we do whatever it is that Christ presents and expects out of us! This is the key point to living a Holy lifestyle. Consider today's prison and the requirements that comes with the sentencing. How your total life is now controlled by this system. Consider how no matter how bad you want a one dollar burger from a certain restaurant you cannot get it. You cannot even see the people that you love so dear whenever you get the urge to. Or, consider how you cannot go outside for fresh air or open a window at your own discretion. Nevertheless, you don't even control the time that you eat and sleep but you must abide and bring your whole entire life under there submission and control. Needless to say you are held bound in a facility that has walls and bars to keep you contained. This is the explanation of becoming a prisoner naturally. However a person becomes a prisoner because of the crime that you have committed and is found guilty, or you are being held in confinement until you are proven innocent. The same stands for a prisoner of Christ. You are guilty of committing sin and Christ has captured you and facilitated you to himself because he has already died and paid for the penalty of your error that you are being charged. He has already set the captives free. But you have pleaded the blood of the Lord Jesus Christ and now you are set free from the chains and bars of sin and are now being transported into the prison of the Lord Jesus Christ. The only difference is that you have no walls or bars that would block you from committing anymore sins. You are covered by the blood of the lamb, sin has no more dominion over your life and you shall now enter into the Kingdom of God once your lifetime prison sentence as a prisoner of Christ is over here on earth. Prisoners of Christ have been found guilty but you have pleaded the blood of the Lord Jesus Christ and now you are not your own but you now belong to the Lord. Your body is now the temple for the Holy Spirit and your soul belongs to God. Finally you are only chosen to be led by the unction of the Holy Spirit.

# MEDITATION

In prison one of the main factors that can be done in your cell is meditation. Meaning access to the outer world is so limited that the only thing left to do is meditate. Meditation requires a very deep thinking process. Remembering those things that we used to do or family and friends that once were in our lives and or how we got to the place where we are at in that time of our life. We begin to ponder on what we could have done to block what caused us to receive this time behind the walls or bars of this man made jail cell. We often feel abandonment and as rejects to the society or real world today! Consider the many feelings of loneliness we would go through on a day to day basis in prison. Missing the very actions that you have always dreamed of once upon a time in your life. The things that we cherish are then taken away from us at once. Listen to me very clearly, there are so many things that trouble your spirit when you remember all of the good times and bad times that made you laugh, smile and cry. You focus mainly on the things that are not there anymore. Then you begin to wish that there were someone who understands you that knew where you have come from in your past life of freedom. Someone who you could compare and share information about things that bothered you the most. This same meditation is needed while you're in the prison of Christ. You must meditate on the word night and day and keep your mind on the Lord Jesus Christ. We must keep our minds on heavenly things which are things above and not below. Constantly thinking about the directions and principles that the Lord has given us to follow. Including each and every precept to get us to the level which God has called us to be on. We must remember that the things of God are contrary to the things and ways of this world. You must keep in mind that God says to be friends with the world is to be an enemy of God. (James 4:4) We must learn his word so that we can know what to do and what not to do. This is something that has to be downloaded into your memory drive of your mind. Proper meditation will keep your mind on kingdom thinking. The things of God and how we should carry out the anointing that he has placed upon our lives with the mindset of Christ. Let this mind be in you which was also in Christ Jesus. (Philippians 2:5) That means to think about situations and things the same way Jesus Christ would think about them. Say the things that he would say as well as walking like Jesus and living the way that he would live. This requires the one on one connection with God. In which the deep meditation will begin to bring you into a prayer life so rich you will be able to obtain the mind of Christ. You will begin to have the wisdom, the knowledge, the understanding, the courage, the power and the authority to carry out his will for your life. Most people who have been delivered and stay delivered from any type of struggle or strong hold are people who meditate and interact with God on a constant basis. Solely alone with just them and God. Getting direction for one's own life. Although the steps of a good man are ordered by the

Lord. (Psalm 37:23) You have to first become a good man; but remember that nobody is good but God. (Mark 10:18) which implies that you must be a Godly man in, order for God to order your steps. A man that is led by the spirit of God and then the spirit that is inside of you will be considered a good man or Godly man. We must continue to meditate on the word both night and day. It is vital for a successful walk on this Christian journey.

# THE MINDSET

When you begin to really think about the place where you are currently at in life, your mind will instantly travel to many of places. If you let your mind know that you are stuck in a prison cell or a trapped closet or maybe even a house with no way out, your mind will began to think how will I survive? What will I do to survive? Is there a way out? How can I break down the walls or the barriers that are holding me down? Is there a legitimate door or gateway out of this cage or prison cell? As a Matter of fact can someone take me to see the judge right now, because I need freedom? These questions will become an attack on the mind, that will create fear and then it leaks down to your heart and transfers over to your emotions. This causes an emotional wreck and frustration that will end up making war with your faith, on surviving in your present situation. Being a prisoner of Christ = Christ like living, would make you oppose this operation of thinking mode with the questions of Godly, like thoughts. Things and questions such as: would Jesus be pleased with me feeling like this? Is this where God wants me, at this point and time of my life? Is this a sign from God? Is this a learning tool that God is using on me? Maybe this is an assignment for me at this time! Is this an opportunity from the Lord to allow me the time to build myself up? Or maybe this is the place that God wants to speak to me? With this mindset of questions on top of having the mind of Christ, you will be able to survive the conquest of the mind. You must pray for the mind of Christ, which is to think how King Jesus the Christ would think; in every situation that you would enter into, in your life. Or, for the new age the better way to think about this is to say WWJD? (What Would Jesus Do?) In which this is a great concept being that the battlefield is of the mind. These four letters WWJD would stick in the corner of your eyes and are very easy to remember. Once you have begun to ask yourself the Godly questions about the situations, while having the mind of Christ. Your Holy Spirit would bring to your memory Godly answers that would help you to encourage yourself in the lord. In spite of the place that you are bound at physically or mentally, the truth of it all is that a Christian is a prisoner of Christ for life. The Apostle Paul also states this matter in the Holy Bible as well. To be a true Christian means that you will change your way of living to the way that Jesus Christ lived when he was here on earth. This emphasizes that one's own mind set is imprisoned to the things of God. That first becomes a mental situation in the inside, transforming the ways of life on the outside of a person. In which the outside is considered the physical part of you. You will then become more susceptible to Godly actions and authority on this earth, as well as prompting and allowing you to carry on this life as a God fearing man or woman. You will not have to worry about how you are going to change these things, because God will do the fixation in your life for you. But you have to allow him the opportunity to make you over, so that he could wash away your sins and make you a new person in Christ. These are the sinful things that are controlling you and they are the exact things that are holding you bound. In which these things do begin in the mind. If you would wake up every morning, praying and asking God to renew your thinking process and remove your old way of thinking this will allow a brand new you to come forth. Consider the apostle Paul's teaching in the book of (Ephesians 4:23-24) and be renewed in the spirit of your mind. And that ye put on the new man, which after God is created in righteousness and true holiness. Also, consider what the prophet Isaiah said in chapter 26:3 Thou wilt keep him in perfect peace, whose mind is stayed on thee: because he trusteth in thee. Which insist that we must trust God with our minds, that he will lead us to the right path and that he would teach us how we should live as Christians. The trouble with allowing God's Holy Spirit to lead us, is that we get impatient and that's when certain thoughts begin to run through our minds that are contrary to having faith in God. The human mind frame is a very important factor in the Christian race because the mind controls the heart and the bible clearly states, "So a man thinketh in his heart so is he" (Proverbs 23). Knowing that the mind controls the body we must keep our minds on things that keeps us in great faith and trusting in God. I cannot express enough for us to refrain from "stinkin thinkin" because it makes us funky! Meaning stay away from bad thoughts, thoughts of failure and things that are not Godly! Finally, brethren, whatsoever things are true, whatsoever things are honest, whatsoever things are just, whatsoever things are pure, whatsoever things are lovely, whatsoever things are of good report; if there be any virtue, and if there be any praise, think on these things (Philippians 4:8).

# RESTRAINING

One must restrain himself from the desires that come to mind. Definitely if they are bad. Sometimes we have to restrain ourselves from good desires and good habits as well. Just because they are good and not contrary to the Holy word of God, does not mean that they are good for you. Or it may not be in Gods will for your life at that present time. With knowing that God knows the end from the beginning his decisions would of course be the very best choice, without a shadow of a doubt. Choosing his choices would bring the outcome that Christ is trying to create in us to come to past in a more sufficient and suitable manner. You should never press against or fight against the will of God, and you should always make it a point to consider Gods will for your life when you are making any decisions. This would cause the very purpose why you were created to be applicable to your life as it will also allow God to get the glory out of your life. For an example I would sometimes find myself acting as if I was a wild dog with a muzzle on my face. Just to help restrain me from saying things that I want to say so bad but yet, I can hear the Holy Spirit saying "don't say anything." That's when you really feel like a prisoner of Christ because you know that it is God telling you to not say nothing at all, even though you already see the mistake that is about to happen.

Sometimes, God allows us to be in prison like situations to help teach us lessons from past mistakes, that will bring on a better you; and for future use. This type of discernment is very vital while you are being taught by God and learning his ways. All the while, we are learning how to be humble and listen and learn from God by his still small voice. This is one of the best ways to learn Gods voice; which is by being in silence, all alone with no contact from any familiar friends or family but only limited to Gods Holy Spirit. Consider how the Prophet Elijah from out of the Holy Bible heard Gods voice.  (1 Kings 19:11-13) (KJV) 11 And he said, Go forth, and stand upon the mount before the Lord. And, behold, the Lord passed by, and a great and strong wind rent the mountains, and brake in pieces the rocks before the Lord; but the Lord was not in the wind: and after the wind an earthquake; but the Lord was not in the earthquake: 12 And after the earthquake a fire; but the Lord was not in the fire: and after the fire a still small voice. 13 And it was so, when Elijah heard it, that he wrapped his face in his mantle, and went out, and stood in the entering of the cave. And, behold, there came a voice unto him, and said, "What doest thou here, Elijah?" Consider how Elijah had listened and heard from God through a still small voice. While "Still" means not moving or making a sound, this is exactly what happens to us when we are imprisoned or restrained. This factor insist, that this is a place and time for us, to be learning how to hear Gods voice while we are getting directions and instructions for our lives. This constant time of restraint will cause clarity and perfection to become a part of our listening skills to God our father. It will also build up our faith, trust in God and our hope as well. I myself like Elijah began to learn his voice by restraining myself from the world with its many of loud noises that it has to offer. Noises like: the television, social networks, social clubs, the radio, friends and family members that presents themselves as distractions. Yes, these are some of the things that I did have to restrain myself from while learning how to hear Gods voice. On the contrary to noises I did however listen to gospel music, attended many of church services and I kept all other noises limited to education upon the word of God. Doing this will then create an atmosphere of praise and worship also it would usher in his Holy Spirit. Remember that the bible informs us that God dwells in the midst of the praises of his people (Psalms 22:3). Now you are not only hearing clearly from God but he has just entered into your place of praise and worship. This is the atmosphere that produces miracles, blessings, his voice, and his very presence while experiencing his glory! This restraint will be considered a much needed position and it is very vital to your journey here on earth.

# A HOSTAGE

A Hostage is a person seized or held as security for the fulfilment of a condition.

As a hostage for the Lord Jesus Christ, we have become captivated to carry out the works of the Kingdome of God here on earth. We are hostages to the will of God and whatever purpose he has chosen to use us for. A hostage is what we should all long for, Christ to bring us unto, instead of captivity to evil ways and sinful desires from Satan and demonic activity. As a hostage you are held without consent or beyond your will, but as a hostage to the Lord Jesus Christ it is not a bad thing. In fact it is remarkably great because, unfortunately we as fleshly men and women sometimes get out of our right minds and get caught up under another spirit. In which would enable us to do the wrong things like walk away from Gods unchanging hand. Although the scripture tells us that no one can pluck you out of Gods hand (John 10:28), yet we can let it go ourselves. Consider (1 Timothy 4:1 KJV) Now the spirit speaketh expressly, that in the latter times some shall depart from the faith, giving heed to seducing spirits, and doctrines of devils. This is why it is a good reason to become a hostage to the Lord Jesus Christ. Consider how hostages present themselves to their unwilling submission to the desires of the required at that time. Also, how they are doing everything they are asked or told to do with fear and trembling. As if their life's total existence depended upon their obedience at that present time. Then consider how every answer coming from them is either yes, yes sir or yes ma'am, sure, no problem, of course and right away. Their actions speak much louder than their words during this time. They live longer when they are obedient to the commands while under captivity, no matter the requirements. As a hostage of the Lord Jesus Christ you will be held as a son of God and you will be set free from the bonds of the enemy. You also are at liberty to serve God in a free manner and is now able to come boldly to the throne of grace that you may obtain mercy and find grace to help in time of need (Hebrews 4:16). The things of God will become pure and natural to you. Things like: truth, love, respect, the fruits of the spirit, caring for others, obedience, seeking after true righteousness, and pure undefiled holiness. Although as hostages we are scared, the good thing about being a hostage to Christ, is that we know that all things work together for the good of those who love the Lord (Romans 8:28). It is the job of a hostage to make sure that the very thing or person that has you bound is pleased with your actions or you are in great jeopardy of facing some kind of punishment or even losing your life. The same thing is needed for Christ's hostages, but the only difference is that it takes faith to please God (Hebrews 11:6). This factor insist that we must believe the very thing that God is telling us that he is going to do for us, if we obey him and trust him. With the mindset that I am a hostage to the Lord Jesus Christ, it would help you to know that you really do belong to someone else who not only truly loves you but also cares and knows exactly where you are at all times. It will have you always looking to the sky or to God to get permission and acceptance for anything that you are uncertain of, if it is in his will for your life. With the Holy Bible telling us to look to the hills from whence comes our help our help comes from the lord which made heaven and earth (Psalms 121:1-2). This will cause us not to stumble and fall as much as we would if we received our every move and directions for our lives from God, and live as if we were hostages to his will. Which would help us to live healthier lives while walking in holiness and not in the pleasures according to our flesh. A hostage to Christ learns to maintain in whatever environment that they are being held in, but yet still not a product of their environment. Meaning although we are in the world we are not supposed to be of it but we are strangers and pilgrims (1Peter 2:11). We must have the same mindset that Gods chosen people had in mind, long before we were here. They lived with the mindset that this was not their home. For we are strangers before thee and, sojourners, as were all our fathers: our days on the earth are as a shadow, and there is none abiding (1Chronicles 29:15).

# SOLITUDE

Solitude- The state or situation of being alone.

Synonyms: loneliness, solitariness, isolation, seclusion, sequestration, withdrawal, privacy, peace

But when you pray, go into your room, close the door and pray to your Father who is unseen. Then your father who sees what is done in secret, will reward you. (Matthew 6:6). Consider when you have something personal to discuss with someone or want to find out some personal information. You would first find a place of seclusion or solitude so that it could be just you and them alone. Then consider the reason why you choose to be alone with that specific person; so that you can find out the truth, the directions and the answers or simply to tell them how you feel. But the fact that no one else is there is really the point that I am trying to make. With that being said, sometimes you have to come into complete solitude in order to achieve certain hurdles or and to become a new person in Christ. The Holy Bible teaches us to tune out or turn down our surroundings in order to hear Gods voice. And once again notice when he spoke to the prophet Elijah he spoke in a still small voice. It was so still that you could have not heard it around a noisy environment. Although, being in solitude puts you by yourself in a lonely place, that lonely place in life is where God comes and meet with you and deals with you personally. It's the time of a personal renewal, edification, instruction and dedication that can take place if you were to go after them with a strong desire. This time is definitely required for those who are seeking to go higher in Christ and to be exactly what God has called them to be. Solitude is that time that you put on your thinking cap and began to plan for the future as God instructs your thoughts and plans. It's time to not only pray, but talk to God and began to learn him on a more personal level and to learn his will for your life. Also, being alone with you and God will give you time to learn the deep things about God and the deep things about yourself that are not on the top surface and things that are not so easily to grasp. It will cause you to triumph every time, because you will be fully aware of the strategy for the plans to properly succeed, in this life of pain, confusion and despair. This type of solitude that I am speaking about should be done at all times for while you are on the Christian journey. I'm not saying abandon your family and friends but I am explaining this scripture out of Gods Holy word from the Bible that states, "be not conformed to this world; but be ye transformed by the renewing of your mind, that ye may prove what is that good, and acceptable, and perfect, will of God" (Romans 12:2). We must change the old thoughts that used to carry us throughout our past lives and lifestyles that managed to help us achieve our past outcomes and set our thinking on things that will help produce our new outcome. This is where being alone will help modify the different influences that will try to distract you from your personal desires. And this one on one with God would also help you with the new thinking pattern that you are trying to develop. We must then become a new person in order to carry out the new things that are needing to be birthed in our lives. In fact Ephesians 4:22-23) tells us to put off concerning the former conversation the old man, which is corrupt according to the deceitful lusts; and be renewed in the spirit of your mind. These kind of thoughts will need to be done in silence and they will require such a deep thinking process that you will practically need to be at a solitude state for this occasion. This time of solitude will allow you to understand what God is saying to you in this current season of your life. It will also enable you to decide on which things that are needed to come through to the steps that are required in your transformation period. Sometimes this along time or solitude is the next step to your transformation that God is trying to convey into your life. The Holy Bible tells us that if any man be in Christ he is a new creature old things has passed away and behold all things are become new. (2Corinthians 5:17) This scripture reassures us that we need to spend alone time with God as often as possible so that we can become what it is that he has called us to be and to be a true man or woman of God. You will also have the true testimony that you are empowered by God and his will for your life as well as proof that you are being led by the Holy Spirit.

# OBEDIENCE

Obedience is better than sacrifice (1Samuel 15:22)

Obedience is a must with God in order for your life's mandate to come forth in its entirety. Being that the Lord is all knowing and knows what's best for us. When he directs you or gives you instructions to do something or gives you ways on how to do it, this would be the best option for you; because God would only send you in the direction that is the best way for you. No matter what it looks like or how it appears to your mind, it is still not so much an option but more of instructions for you.

Which would in the end, get you closer to the call on your life or the reason for your very existence. Keep in mind that the Lord told us that his ways are not our ways and his thoughts are not our thoughts (Isaiah 55: 8-9). This statement signifies that our plans or our outlooks on different situations in our lives may not be exactly what God has planned out for us. This also could mean the way that we perceive certain things or somethings that we think that are okay, they may not line up to God's will for our lives. Those things that are not lining up with God's directions or if we fail to follow God's instructions, could actually lead us into a ditch or a detour from the road that God is trying to lead us on. I believe that obedience to God is equal to living on purpose. I also believe that If we really love the Lord and would like to show it to God, Jesus said keep or obey his commandments

(John 14:15). Now therefore, if ye will obey my voice indeed, and keep my covenant, then ye shall be a peculiar treasure unto me above all people: for all the earth is mine: And ye shall be unto me a kingdom of priests, and a holy nation (Exodus 19:5-6). God has instructed me to be obedience and that is how I have made it to where I am today. God instructs my every move in my life, when I chose to listen and obey him; and as a result I am now walking towards and in my deliverance process from my past and present life's struggles. I truly believe that God has presented those who obey him with a life after death coupon as well as life more abundantly while living here on earth as well. Righteously speaking we become deprived in our own lives when we are walking in disobedience to God. The same way that Adam was deprived and dismissed from the Garden of Eden and then summoned to death because of his disobedience. In which he has now caused all humanity to have to die just like him. I feel that if Adam would have obeyed God, he would most likely still be here today. Adams story was an example to the world what would happen to all humanity when we began to be disobedient to God. I remember when I first started obeying Gods Holy word and his voice. He had then begun ordering my every foot step and everything in my life did began to fall into place. My life had begun to now make sense to me. Yes, friends got few and things did too but the inward man began to come through and I had begun to live from the inside out. The joy was unspeakable from within! Laughter was frequent while bitterness and resentment was far away too! We would be able to be incarcerated by Gods will for our lives If we, cast down imaginations, and every high thing that exalteth itself against the knowledge of God, and bring into captivity every thought to the obedience of Christ (2 Corinthians 10:5). Blessed rather are those who hear the word of God and obey it (Luke 11:28). If we really think about it, whatever it is that we choose to obey is our God and our guide, as well as it sets the standards for our everyday living practices. So, if we set in our hearts and minds the word of God, these are the things that we would exactly do and it would set the standards for our living arrangements and practices daily. This is why I CHOOSE to obey God and his holy word because I am living out the true meaning of a Christian or Christ like way of living. As Christians we must live according to the word of God and not the urges from our flesh or live by the ways that the world live by. In spite of our fleshly urges and of everything that you see with the many of life's temptations we must continue on in obedience to God. Consider how the word explains how Jesus was yet God but was fashion as a man, he still humbled himself, and became obedient unto death, even the death of the cross (Philippians 2:8). We must live our lives the same way in obedience until our final hour here on earth comes. So that when we get to the crossroads, we will see Jesus face to face and he will tell us well done my good and faithful servant. But in order to hear him say that, we must be doing good and living out the lifestyle of a faithful obedient true servant of God.

Song:  **<u>I Surrender All</u>**

All to Jesus I surrender;

All to Him I freely give;

I will ever love and trust him,

In his presence daily live.

Refrain:

I surrender all,

I surrender all;

All to thee, my blessed Savior,

I surrender all.

All to Jesus I surrender;

Humbly at his feet I bow,

Worldly pleasures all forsaken;

Take Me Jesus, take me now.


All to Jesus I surrender;

Make me, Savior, wholly thine;

Let me feel the Holy Spirit,

Truly know that thou art mine.


All to Jesus I surrender;

Lord, I give myself to thee;

Fill me with thy love and power;

Let thy Blessing fall on me.


All to Jesus I surrender;

Now I feel the sacred flame.

Oh, the joy of full salvation! Glory, Glory, to his name!

# HANDS UP (SURRENDER)

Hands up means everything that you have in your hands and in your total possession have to be put down willingly, or another way to say this is to say "I surrender". When it comes to living this Christian race we must surrender all to God in order to fully submit ourselves to him. If we empty out ourselves and what we have in our hands, God can then fill us up with his power and put the things in our hands that he desires for us to have and work with. Although we are justified by grace we do not have to worry about doing things the wrong way or our outcome, if our hearts are led and controlled by the Holy Spirit; being the Holy

Spirit will never mislead us. The Holy Bible teaches us that the Holy Spirit will lead us into all truth (John 16:13). Remember that the steps of a good man or ordered by the Lord: and he delights in his way (Psalm 37:23). We should totally hand our little lives over to God so that he can show us how much bigger he is and how much better things would work out for us with God in total control. Keep in mind the scripture that states, my thoughts are not your thoughts and my ways are not your ways, declares the Lord. For as the heavens are higher than the earth, so are my ways higher than your ways and my thoughts than your thoughts (Isaiah 55:8-9). We could never get our minds to understand what it is to know what God is thinking for us, but the only thing that we are sure of is that God said in his holy word that he knows the thoughts that he thinks towards us and that they are of peace and not of evil, to give us an expected end (Jeremiah 29:11). We must trust God with every part of our lives and the things that surrounds it. The moment that we do this, things will begin to shift in our favor and begin to instantly reveal that a higher power has placed his touch onto our situation. Family and friends will see the major change in your life and begin to wonder and seek who and what it is that you are doing that's causing such a major blessing in your life. Your light begins to shine so bright that it can even be seen in areas that are created to block you. Surrendering ourselves to God as a whole will also reveal who's Lord of our lives and who's in total control of our lives. Why try to figure out what we are supposed to do and what we are created to be when we can go to our creator and be put into our rightful place and be led by him. The

Holy Bible states that in all your ways acknowledge him and he shall direct your path (Proverbs 3:6). This means that we must surrender everything to him and let him know that we are giving him charge of our lives and everything in it, that not only he would get the glory but also he will make sure that we are well taken care of. I have been young and now am old; yet have I not seen the righteous forsaken, nor his seed begging for bread (Psalms 37:25). When we empty out ourselves to God and allow him to lead us, he will lead us on the path of righteousness and it would also help us to stay in tuned with God; as it would continue to keep things on a constant flow with his will for our lives. That very moment that we fall off of track or get confused on which way to go and the feeling of total despair begins to rise, it would be a good time to get into a place in your mind and heart that says; "ok God, I'm finish trying to do it myself and I'm done with trying to work this out!" Then take our little hands off of the situation and let the Lord do his job and watch the outcome turn out better than it would have been, even if we were able to do it ourselves. Most of the time God allows the feeling of being confused, lost and giving up to come about, so that we could give him the opportunity to show himself in our needs and our lives period. He often does this to reveal that he is able to do all things, that he is a loving and caring God and that he still knows what's best for you even when you are lost yourself. Letting go and letting God in every situation would be the best decision because it would first give you comfort that everything is going to work out properly and according to his plans. And on the other hand it would also give you a testimony to tell the world how

God has brought you out and have done this great thing for you. God specializing in the impossible is a known factor and not just from the stories in the Holy Bible but also according to the lives who are yet alive today. We should have learned at a certain age that it was God who stepped in and fought many of our battles for us, seen and unseen. So, just imagine if you gave up everything freely and told God that you wanted him to take total control for not just this one situation but for every situation that comes in your life. There will then be a lifestyle created in you that is of peace and not worrying about life's many of difficulties. In fact there is an old hymn called, "I Surrender All" that is sung in several different ways in most church's no matter the denomination. Consider some of the words that are sung in that particular hymn and how they pertain to dealing with worldly things that we have forsaken for Christ. There is a place that we get to in our lives where most of us will still hold on to things that we should not and yet give God just a piece of us; when God is simply instructing us to let it go, not some but all. When doing this it causes unnecessary stress and strife that we do not have to go through, just because we are sons and daughters of the creator of all things. Although, it is a feeling of fear that comes to test your faith in God when surrendering and putting our hands up, this feeling or spirit will not triumph over you. Just have faith in God for, I Antwan Amey, am a living witness that if you hand it over to him he will see you through and you will not be disappointed because you have surrendered it all to God. Put your hands up and surrender!

# OWN RECOGNIZANCE (O.R.)

Thy word have I hidden in my heart that I might not sin against thee (Psalms 119:11). This particular scripture explains the O.R. Own recognizance because it is a bail out that does not cost you anything but the decisions that you make inside. It simply enlightens your insides on things, thoughts or plans that does not line up with the word of God. God's Holy word must be inside of you so that when you yourself begin to make choices that are unlawful there will be a conviction that will take place immediately. If you still make that choice it will be all your fault and no one else, because the Holy Spirit or God's word will let you know the choice that you are choosing to make. Even if someone prompts you to do the wrong thing or even try to convince or persuade you, it will not work. The bible simply teaches us that out of the heart flows the issues of life (Proverbs 4:23). That means the heart is the area of our bodies where we harvest our cares and things that really matters or things that we love so dear. Proverbs 4:23 also teaches us to keep our hearts with all diligence. Therefore if we put Gods word in our heart and leave it there when the issues of life come the word would saturate the way that we perceive the issues, if they are present in the heart; being that's where the issues are kept. Notice how God's word is always fighting against the things that are contrary to him and his word. Notice how before your able to make infallible choices that your heart is already prompt to deal with it in a Godly manner. This is one of the most important known facts that helps Christians to remain in the Christian race. Well, for me at least! We must read, study and learn God's Holy Word! For it is a lamp for my feet, a light on my path (Psalm 119:105). It's like going grocery shopping and buying food to store up for later on when you become hungry. This will allow you to eat whenever the hunger starts to bother you by feeding it with what you already have in stored. Also, when you hide the word in your heart it acts as if it is a vaccination unto the sinful things that tries to enter into us, by reminding us of God's Holy word. Thy word have I hid in mine heart, that I might not sin against thee (Psalms 119:11). When the sin nature begins to rise off inside of you or it comes at you by way of thoughts, people, places, or things, Gods Holy word begin to make you think to yourself these things: I cannot do this, God will not be pleased with me, or I know this has nothing about it that is righteousness or holiness at all and it is contrary to the rules and God's laws for my life! It is the word of God that really enlightens us on the do's and don'ts for our path on this Christian road of life. For the word of God is quick, and powerful and sharper than any two edged sword, piercing even to the dividing asunder of soul and spirit, and of the joints, and marrow, and is a discerner of the thoughts and intents of the heart (Hebrews 4:12). Notice how the scripture enlightens us on how the word is a divider of soul and spirit which it literally prompts you to know the difference in the good from the bad of every situation that may try to come our way. In which is normally sent by Satan that old serpent who is also known as the tempter and the accuser of the brethren. His job is to steal, kill and destroy or better yet he is basically trying to make you slip and fall and give up on God and completing this Christian race. So that hopefully you will not make it to the final destination which is heaven because he himself got kicked out. God had already fore known this, so he equipped us by giving us an escape route by way of his Holy word, that would cause the tricks and fiery darts of Satan not to work or that would cause us not to stumble. Use your own recognizance (O.R) to bail yourself out of worthless decision making.

# TIMED SERVED

There is therefore now no condemnation to them which are in Christ Jesus (Romans 8:1).

We have to be careful during this particular time of our lives because the enemy will try his best to keep you in bondage. Starting with the bondage in your mind first and then he will try to keep you in bondage physically and spiritually, if we do not keep ourselves grounded in God and his holy word. You must first start this journey with the mindset that this is what I was called to do and stick to it, in-spite of the circumstance that may present itself to you. You must change your mind from all negative things that you were used to thinking about in the past and place your mind on the bigger, brighter and positive goals that you are trying to achieve in life, right now! Basically, we must remain from "Stinkin Thinkin!" Most things that we do in our lifetime starts with a thought first, then we react and play on whatever it is that we have been thinking about or meditating on. If you really dwell on whatever it is that you are thinking so deeply about, you will then cause yourself to bring this thought to past immediately or as soon as possible. In spite of how hard or how far away it may be, you will try everything you know in your mind to help bring this specific task to par. Imagine riding past your favorite restaurant and you begin to think about that favorite chocolate chip cookie that you love to eat. You begin to remember how it taste and how it had pleased your taste buds and your belly so well. If you think about it so much and dwell on it you will end up in that restaurant purchasing it. Our mind controls our body for the most part and essentially the body will respond to the mind. So, if we pray to keep our minds on Christ Jesus we will be able to focus on the things that he desires for us. As a matter of fact the Holy Bible teaches us to pray to let the mind that was in Christ Jesus also be in us (Philippians 2:5). Therefore with this mindset we will set our atmosphere to obtain the things of God on a continuous and daily choice: for it is a self-sacrificial decision. We have to be fully persuaded that Jesus Christ is the son of God and that we are called to live a lifestyle of sacrifice, just like Jesus did. Next, you will have to read his Holy word, by studying and learning how God works and what is the difference between the Godly and ungodly things. Then you would download all of this information into your brain or mind and when you begin to meditate on the word or the things of God you will began to enjoy these things. Truthfully, at the beginning they will be a challenge and some of them will not be choices that you were used to doing or obeying. Once you have become prone to the things of God you will be able to know and recognize the things of God anywhere you go. Then you will be able to get to know the things that God desires for you to not only be around but the people and places that are out of place for you or things that you should not be around. It will become natural for you to obey unction of the Holy Spirit or Gods will for your life. Now, your hangout spots and your social networks will have a great impact and influence on your life's journey because they will be things of God. They will either shape you, make you or break you into the person of your character as well as impact the way that you carry yourself. The total objective in this life is to become more and more like Christ. To live a life that is Holy and acceptable unto God which is our reasonable service (Romans 12:1). Yes, we will make many mistakes because we are not perfect but the bible teaches us to become perfected in the way that we live. Even with that we are still not good because the bible also teaches us that no one is good but God alone (Mark 10:18). With that being said, Christ's obedience until the cross and his resurrection, including his blood has already paid the cost for us. Which means that our time for our penalty has already been served.   Hallelujah!!!

# YOUR CREATED TESTIMONY

Coming out of darkness or being considered set free creates a process of deliverance. Even if it's nothing but going through the different mindsets that it takes to not only become free but also to remain free. We must remember that deliverance is not just a process with different stages and a new mindset but it's also a lifelong decision that we have to make on a day to day basis. The Holy Bible states that we must be renewed in our minds daily (Romans 12:2). That's because becoming a Christian is more than just being baptized in Jesus name and being filled with the Holy Spirit. It's more than just getting up on Sundays and going to the church running, jumping, screaming or shouting. But it's a lifestyle that we must choose to live with a joyous spirit. Meaning we must approach this situation with compassion and love. Also, with knowing that this is what your new lifestyle consist of but also with the demeanor that I am doing this for Christ. With the mind frame that I am bringing God's kingdom down to earth. People must be able to see the God in you so that you can be a living testimony to God changing you on the inside and out. In fact this entire time while you are going through these stages in your life you are developing your testimony. Many of the things that you must change and overcome in these stages, will create an experience that will make you a new creature in Christ. Everyone will notice your change and some will also acknowledge the new you and begin to witness to others how God has come into your life and transformed it for the good. This then becomes a form of witness and ministry that will become automatically applied to your life, just because of your impression that you are giving off. You have just received a valid testimony that the world can see clearly! Specifically to non- Christian believers and people like your close friends and family members that knew who you were and how you used to carry yourself; but they will have recognized how far God has brought you. They have even watched many of the different phases that God has brought you through, to get you to your deliverance process in order to create your life long testimony. In which the Holy Bible said that we overcome by the blood of the lamb and by the word of our testimony (Revelation 12:11). This insist that we will be able to make it into heaven by first the blood of the Lord Jesus Christ that washed away all of our sins. All the while, we are being delivered from that sin that so easily besets us. Which will be one of our biggest testimonies once God has totally delivered us from whatever that sin is that is hindering your freedom, your witness and your testimony. As you are living this lifestyle as an agent of change you are also writing your own chapter or testimony into the Holy Bible. Remember that some people will only get a chance to read your chapter of the Holy Bible, so we must make sure that it is authentic and God driven. Most importantly it must consist of a lifestyle of transformation, being we were all born into sin and shapen by iniquity (Psalms 51:5). This will alert the current sinners that we are sinners as well but we are sinners that are saved by grace and are now saints that have been adopted into to the family of God through the Lord Jesus Christ. That we are now a chosen generation, a royal priesthood, a holy nation, a peculiar people; that we should shew forth the praises of him who hath called us out of darkness into his marvelous light (1Peter 2:9). We must keep in mind that we have to live this lifestyle of complete holiness at all times. Because there are people who are watching us and people that God has sent our way, to learn how to live a lifestyle as a Christian, just from watching our everyday living. There obviously could not be a testimony without a test that you must past or achieve the completion for accomplishing your goal. Whatever sin or the sin nature that God has revealed to you that is constantly causing you to fall is considered your test. But you are not the only person who has that particular sin issue, because there are many of people who have that same down fall that will need to know and to be enlightened on how God delivered you and set you free from this same test. This is why one of my favorite scriptures is, "And when you have been converted, strengthen thy brethren" (Luke 22:32). In order to accomplish a goal there must be boundaries and margins that must be set. But the most important one of them all is, not to stop until we have completed the entire task. Consider you are running a race and you have just tripped and fell over your own shoe. You may have scraped your knee with a wound on the side of it, but you must get up and continue running this race and cross the finish line. In order for you to really say that you have completed this race. Do not wave the white flag of surrender or turn around and leave the race but you must keep going until you cross that finish line. This is the same attitude that you must have when running this Christian race, being the Holy Bible refers to this lifestyle of Christianity as a race. Do you not know that those who run in a race all run, but only once receives the prize? Run in such a way that you may win. Everyone who competes in the games exercises self-control in all things they then do it to receive a perishable wreath, but we an imperishable. Therefore I run in such a way, as not without aim; I box in such a way, as not beating the air; but I discipline my body and make it my slave, so that, after I have preached to others, I myself will not be disqualified (1Corinthians 9:24-27 NKJV). You Christians are now a living testimony of the Lord Jesus Christ and representation of the Kingdom of God here on earth.

# BACK TO THE FUTURE

Once we have become incarcerated into any prison our minds sometimes elapse and remember what our future dreams and goals were. We are reminded that in a place of imprisonment our hopes and dreams seems to be over or at the very least too far away to achieve. This kind of thinking can cause an attack upon the mind that makes you lose hope in your future and yourself. It makes you feel like you really do not care about living anymore. This is a mindset that persuades you to believe that life has dealt you a bad hand or sour lemons forever. The voices of the people who once told you that your dreams would not come true, will begin to replay in your mind. All of the doubters and haters words, begin to suppress the truth that you had believed in. Now, you have no one and nothing there to push you towards creating the lifestyle that you had desired. In fact, everyone that you will have to encounter will most likely have the same situation going on in their lives as well. Being that everyone there is in prison and under the same rules, most likely they will have the same concept going on in their minds. This concept develops a mental mind frame that sometimes causes you to adapt to your environment and the living arrangements that are in place at that time. It's safe to say that you have now become a product of your environment. This is what exactly takes place when you surround yourself on things of God and Godly rules that governs over all Christians. When you turn your environment into a Christian environment you will began to see your atmosphere and mindset shift to things of holiness. But this will take your thought pattern back to your dreams and visions that you had set for yourself, when you were planning for your future life style. This thinking process will take you back to the things that you had always desired to do, and will enable you to seek God on questions like: How do I get to the place that I am trying to go? And what are the steps that are needed for you to accomplish your dreams. As a matter of fact you will be able to find out from him if they are even a part of the journey that he has laid out before you to complete. God knows exactly what it is that he is preparing you for and when you are going to arrive to that place, and also the road that is going to lead you there. The word tells us that; whom he did foreknow, he also did predestinate to be conformed to the image of his son, that he might be the firstborn among many brethren. Moreover whom he did predestinate, them he also called: and whom he called, them he also justified: and whom he justified, them he also glorified (Romans 8:29-30). I personally believe that God always installs in us the things that we will be or the things that we should be working towards becoming from a very early age. Reason being is because, he must equip us with the right tools and people to get us to that very place called, destination. No it's not always true that we know God's total plan for our future lives or even the route to take to get there but there would be at the very least some signs, gifts and talents that will be present in our earlier stages of life. In which they would create the path that is needed for the destination. Then there will be tools that will began to develop us as we continue to live and grow both in body and in wisdom just as the Lord Jesus Christ did (Luke 2:52). This will enable you to have a strong finish because you would have developed strong faith in God, while believing that he will carry out every promise that he has given you. When knowing that there is no good thing that he will withhold from them who walk uprightly (Psalm 84:11). You will now have developed a sense to know what's right and what's wrong for you and who is good for your path and who is not. A strong discernment will become developed in you while you are in this particular mind frame as a prisoner of Christ. The reminiscing of all of the good things that you have planned for in the future, will take you back to the places that you were in when you began to form these places and goals that you were desiring to achieve. Believe me the place where you are when you are now re-planning these goals and dreams will make you feel like you are in a prison cell with a long journey in front of you. Although this may be true, we often forget these things and the very places that you are trying to achieve while on the way there. Mainly because of life's difficulties and the pressure that it takes while trying to present your body as a living sacrifice, holy and acceptable unto God which is our reasonable service (Romans 12:1). Sometimes we have to go back to our future dreams and goals to remind us what we are trying to accomplish and become while we are here on earth, but if we lose focus it could cause us to fall out of place or the order of steps to get us to our desired destination. This imprisonment of Christ will bring our memory back to the place where God has showed us and allowed our dreams and visions to reveal our very destination in this thing called life.

# FROM A BOOK TO A FRIEND

I was told that the word Bible stands for-
Basic, Instructions, Before, leaving, Earth. At
least that's what I have always been taught.
I have actually agreed to this conception
after re-reading the Holy Bible over and
over again. I considered how I would use
this book as a reference guide to how,
what, when, and where I was supposed to
carry out this thing called life; in a Godly
manner. I begin to notice that the words
that I was reading were very significant to
the things that I was seeking for and the
encouragement that was needed for
everyone else. I believe if we would take

the time to read it with understanding and compassion it will be a compass for our lives. The book will then become a part of your everyday thinking process and your guide to surviving here on earth. Most importantly it begins to take you to the next level, in which is the spirit realm or spiritual level. Once you have been filled with the baptism of the Holy Spirit and have begun to walk in the spirit you will began to come into contact with your creator, which is through Jesus Christ. Jesus will begin to reveal and manifest himself unto you, through many of different ways. Next, he will begin to treat you as the person of your greatest dreams, as he will also become the friend or family member that you were always yearning for. In fact, he is the perfect source to all humanity. His holy words in the bible will be one of our main resources to him. The Holy Bible is a book that literally lives and supplies the necessary nutrients for life yesterday, today and forever more; by faith. Being that the words in the Holy Bible are Holy Spirit inspired, (which equals Gods words); the bible states that heaven and earth may pass away but my words shall never pass away (Matthew 24:25). These things gives us an understanding that Gods words are living and they are proceeding from the mouth of God and now they just need a face with them. To bring better knowledge of who and what are stating these words and orchestrating these things of the spirit. The bible then begins to teach us that God has a son whom name is Jesus and that, it was him that has been given power over everything (Luke 1:35) (John 5:20/ 3:16). The bible then makes it known that God wrapped himself up in flesh and came down to fulfill his own requirement as a self-sacrifice who is Jesus, in which Jesus was the only perfect and acceptable sacrifice. Now, we should be most certain that God is in Christ and Christ is in him (John 14:10). Yet we should know God as more than just a fable in a book or a fairy tale that reminds you of a genie in a bottle. But we should at the very least know him to be someone who shows up for us when we least expect it and is always there. As a matter of fact we should know him for specializing in the impossible and the un-thinkable because I'm pretty sure that there has been plenty of times that we have gotten ourselves into situations. Where we did not know what we were going to do or how we were going to get out of them, but God showed up and showed out just for us. Even when we had not been our very best and did not deserve it but he still manages to show up for us and solve whatever issue it was. This did not only get our attention at this time but this was an understanding that came from an accumulation of times where God has revealed himself in our situations, where we knew for a fact that it could have not been anyone else but God. With this feeling or understanding you begin to want more of him, in fact it draws you to a deeper relationship and a higher level of trust with him. This is where we begin to recognize that we have a friend in God through Jesus Christ! For an example, this is when we begin to tell others how God has showed up and treated us like, one of our old relationships where we thought we could trust them but somehow they ended up letting us down at the end; for whatever reason that we were trusting them to fulfill in our lives. You begin talking about God to your friends and family here on earth as if you have just met a new trust worthy friend or family member. You then begin to try to talk to him and tell him every day thank you for this and explaining to him that you know that he is real and not only real but real in your life as well. You also begin to love on him as he continues to open up windows and doors for you that you least expect for him to open. This will prompt your emotions and mind to begin to understand I do have a friend that sticks closer than a brother and someone who really does care and can be there no matter how late or early it is. You begin to talk to him on a day to day basis but not just to remind him of your everyday issues and worries but also to express how grateful you are to have met a friend such as him. You have now entered into a new zone that creates a relationship status that sets a platform for you to say that I am a friend of God and he is a friend of mine. This is when you have brought the words of that book the Holy Bible to life, to truth, to reality and have brought it from a book to a friend!

Poem:

# A FATHER IS:

Love, a provider, a comforter, a peace maker, wisdom at its best, a trouble shooter,

a supplier, a help, a fighter for you, a creator, he is hope, he is joy, he is very courageous, he is skilled, a

believer in you, a shoulder to lean on, a tissue for your tears, eyes for you, a counselor, a ride or die, a

partner, he is justice, a maker of you, an idol to you, a promise keeper, a source, a king, a man, a warrior, a knight and shining armor, the tool, a way maker, a friend, a healer, a parent,

a light in light and darkness, a judge, a miracle worker, a brain, a dream, a delight, he is everything, he is alive, he is a God,

For me he is my Lord and Savior

Jesus The Christ!

# A SON NOW

As children who are loved by their father's you have a peculiar relationship with each other. You can ask them for anything and they will make sure they do what they can to satisfy their children, even if it means a substitution for whatever it is. On the other hand the child will try their best to do the same for the father and his desires, to the best of the child's ability. The relationship is so respected that things are not really complicated they are understanding and are on an agreeable level. This does not mean that the decisions will always be seen eye to eye but the child will trust and know that the father has the best interest for the child and direction for their life. Being that parents are the first role models for their children, the children will always keep into consideration the path that their parents desired for their lives. With this being said, God wants all of his chosen ones to receive him as their father. Which would make all of us sons and daughters of God to them who proclaims him to be their father. But we need to accept him as this person and not just a wide brand of different things that the world may try to tell us what God is to us. Mainly because he is actually more than just those things that they have experienced him to be in their lives. Things like: a doctor, lawyer, teacher, provider and anything else that they could call him according to the things that he supplies them with, that they cannot get or do themselves, here on earth. Consider what a father is- a man in relation to his natural child or children. This really explains who God is to each and every one of us whom consider him their father. Just a little piece of Gods character explains just the meaning of what a father is. Which insist that he is not only our father but everything else that we could possibly think of. This also explains what the Holy bible means when it refers to God as "I Am"! Because everything that you think of or could even imagine or need God is. Why not consider him as your father when he is not only your creator but the creator of everyone and everything. Now, with this being said when you come into the mind frame that God is your father and that you are his son/daughter, you will begin to treat him in a different manner. Most importantly you will begin to treat yourself differently and live in a Godly manner. Living like the child of the king or living like this is your father's earth and everything on it, because it really is. This way of thinking will create a new way of living that will enhance not only the very presence of God your father in your life but it would also enhance the things that you would do and be while living here on earth. Referring to God as your father will also put you in the mindset that if there is anything that is lacking or if we are confused of which way to go, surely we could just ask our father because he is not lacking in any way or confused about anything. In fact sometimes as fathers it feels good to have your child to come to you for direction especially when you are the provider and the immediate source to your child's total being. With this reality we should never feel lost or down and out because we know that our father will never leave his child hopeless or lost. As a young son or daughter we were always expecting our parents to take care of us and to provide our every need as long as we needed them, until we had gotten to an age of self- supporting. This is how we should feel once we have the true understanding of who and what God really is to us, through the Lord Jesus Christ. Most issues that are causing our lives to be so destructive and misleading us to the feeling of despair and giving up is because of the things that we lack in life or what we would consider the necessities of life. But with God as our father who is the author and finisher of our faith (Hebrews 12:2) we should never feel like this or even allow anyone we know or come into contact with to feel this way. My people perish for the lack of knowledge (Hosea 4:6). Maybe this is one of the many of reasons that God had put this in his word. Mainly, because of our failure to know that we could come to him for anything and he would speak to us about that exact situation at hand. With the revelation on how to come out of that situation also with the best option to choose. We must apprehend this idea as being a son of God so that we could live a life that is satisfying to us and pleasing to him. This would also calm down the stress level in our society today because of the consistent lack of needs not being met, because of the lack of authority over the necessities that life calls for, that only God can supply. If we would honor God as our father he is able to supply all of our needs according to his riches in glory by Christ Jesus (Philippians 4:19)! One of my favorite aunts Vera told me that if you would consider him as your father and let him know that you are leaning and depending on him, he would come through for you when you are least expecting him too. This kind of faith is what moves our God but its knowing him at a level of a close relationship at all times and not just when you are in a bind, where he is only the other option to creating a way out of your circumstance. We should be on a level with him where we are representing him as sons and daughter and referring to him as our daddy or our father in heaven. I personally refer to God as my daddy because it reveals that our relationship is closer than just that as a father or birth parent. It actually reflects the relationship that we have that carries on a day to day basis as my true daddy would have been to me, if he was still here today. With considering God as our father and we as his children we can now live a lifestyle of total Victory!

# INVISIBLE CHAINS (PRAYER)

Touch no unclean thing, and I will receive you (2Corinthians 6:17)

Invisible chains will keep you from touching things that you should not touch. I remember saying a prayer in my prayer room that went like this:

Father in the mighty name of Jesus I ask you to help me to stay away from things that are not clean. Things that are not good for me and things that are hazardous to my life. Lord remove anything that's not like you out of my reach, out of my view and keep me chained and bound to your blessings. Keep my mind from thinking of those things that are contrary to your holiness. Keep my mouth from speaking those things into existence and remove the past memory from all sorts of evilness, wicked devices, drugs, alcohol and sexual perversion. Father I ask that you bound me to your ways and place before me the things that you desire for me to touch and bring into my life. Lord thank you for your head of protection as you continue to keep me in the time of temptation that it may not over take me. Thank you for strength when I am weak and setting up a standard for when the enemy comes in like a flood, that he cannot touch me. Thank you Lord for keeping me even when I didn't want to be kept and for blocking the tricks and schemes of the enemy and his wicked influences. Now Lord I ask you to continue to keep me and to allow your voice and the unction of the Holy Spirit to lead, guide and protect me in my everyday life. Thank you for the wisdom to be wise enough to know and to understand the things that are of God and the things that are not of God. Help me to live my life as a prisoner of Christ and respecting my temple (body) from the unclean things. Thank you Lord for self-control over my flesh as I continually renew my mind daily. In Jesus matchless name I pray.

Amen!!!

# NOW UNTO HIM WHO IS ABLE TO KEEP YOU FROM FALLING, AND TO PRESENT YOU FAUTLESS BEFORE THE PRESENCE OF HIS GLORY WITH EXCEEDING JOY!

## (JUDE 1:24)

## APOSTLE ANTWAN AMEY

The Apostle Antwan Amey is the author and publisher of "The Totality Of Deliverance." He is now releasing his newest book called, "Christ's Prison Has No Bars." Antwan is 33 years of age and lives in the great city of Indianapolis, Indiana, where he is an astonishing writer and preparer of Gods Holy word! He is a chosen servant and son for the Lord Jesus Christ, dedicated and fully committed to the works of the Kingdom of God. With Antwan's life changing experience and his journey with the Lord Jesus Christ; his purpose is to win as many souls as possible for Christ, help set the bound souls free and build up Gods Kingdom here on earth. Antwan enjoys inspiring the people in the world today as his books will be one of the many of resources that he will use, to win the souls!

# The Editor

Stephanie Coleman my cousin, my favorite and my editor! Once again she has been such a major blessing to me. Stephanie is an early childhood educator, a loving mother and devoted wife that has her hands tied up but yet, still makes time to edit my books. I truly thank God for her talent, wisdom, knowledge and her expertise that she shows during this process. I would also like to thank her husband L.C and her children for allowing her the time to really get into detail and present me a perfected, edited, book. Thanks Stephanie and once again you help make dreams come true! I Love You!

ORDER YOUR BOOK TODAY!

# THE TOTALITY OF DELIVERANCE!

No matter what curse is upon your life, God can totally deliver you from them all!

Antwan Amey explains:
- How to be set free from Sexual Perversion?
- That there is repentance for Homosexuality?
- Reveals **THE PHASES TO THE DELIVERANCE PROCESS** and more!

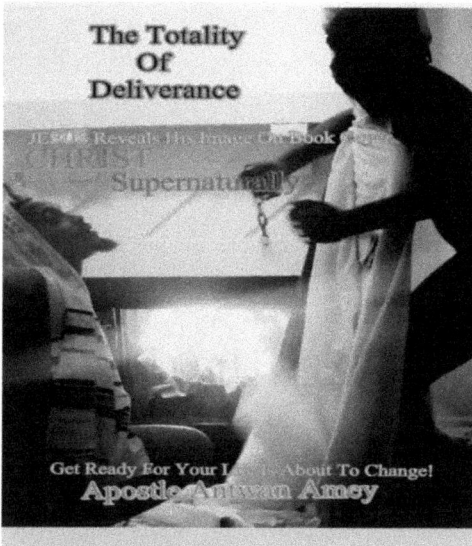

# The Lord Jesus Christ Super Naturally Reveals his Image On Front Cover!

Available Online- www.amazon.com / www.createspace.com / Kindle
Apostle ForChrist Antwan Amey @Facebook